SECRETS

SECRETS

Helen Dunmore

The Bodley Head
LONDON

1 3 5 7 9 10 8 6 4 2

Copyright © Helen Dunmore 1994

Helen Dunmore has asserted her right under the Copyright, Designs
and Patents Act 1988 to be identified as the author of this work

First published in the United Kingdom 1994
by The Bodley Head Children's Books
Random House, 20 Vauxhall Bridge Road, London SW1V 2SA

Random House Australia (Pty) Limited
20 Alfred Street, Milsons Point, Sydney,
New South Wales 2061, Australia

Random House New Zealand Limited
18 Poland Road, Glenfield,
Auckland 10, New Zealand

Random House South Africa (Pty) Limited
PO Box 337, Bergvlei 2012, South Africa

Random House UK Limited Reg. No. 954009

A CIP catalogue record for this book is available from the
British Library

ISBN 0 370 31882 X

Phototypeset by Intype, London
Printed in Great Britain by
Mackays of Chatham Plc, Chatham, Kent

CONTENTS

Night Cat	9
Country Darkness	10
Yellow	12
Harbour Seal	13
Breeze of Ghosts	14
Wolf in My Pocket	15
Secret Forest	16
Night Lorries	18
Lorries Behind	19
Sad Lorries	19
The Cuckoo Game	20
Whooper Swans	21
Russian Doll	23
Snow Queen	24
The Bones of the Vasa	26
The Braggart and the Pudding	27
Marks	32
Roper	33
Jim Bean	35
Jim Bean and the Swifts	37
Jim Bean and the Darkness of Heaven	38
Christmas Caves	39
For Francesca	40
Playground Haiku	41
Baby Orang-utan	41
Freewheeling	42

Lemon Sole	43
Hedgehog Hiding at Harvest in Hills Above Monmouth	44
Waterlily	46
My List Of Night	47
Herring Girl	49
The Buried Medal	51
The Butcher's Daughter	52
Small Dip in the Stone	54
Me Missing a Party	55
The Pelting Rain	57
The Catherine Wheel Whinge	58
White Moon	59
The Greenfield Ghost	60
That Violet-Haired Lady	61
Winter Haiku	62
Richard the Bad, Richard the Good	63
Pomegranates Do Not Feel Pain	64

A LETTER FROM THE AUTHOR

Hidden worlds. They are everywhere, around us and inside us. These poems take you under the skin, behind the mask, through the locked door. They are about searching beneath the surface of what is around you. Look at something as simple as a hair or a drop of blood under a microscope, and see how magical it becomes. Or try to understand the dreams and hopes behind another person's eyes.

In one poem you'll follow in the footsteps of a homeless boy through the long night and find out why dawn is the coldest time. In another, you'll watch a baby orang-utan clutch its mother's fur and guess what it sees when it looks back at you. At any time an ordinary day can become extraordinary. You're standing by a harbour wall and suddenly a seal breaks the surface with its black nose, then dives again to its secret life beyond the smell of burgers and the waves slapping against the sides of the fishing boats. Or you look out of the car's rear window and see that the metal grille of the juggernaut at your bumper is like a row of bared teeth. There are ghosts in these poems too, which reflect the hidden life of the past. Ghosts of green fields now covered by housing estates, the ghost of a slave ship abandoned by its captain, the ghost of a butcher's daughter who wanted to choose what she'd do with her own life.

Many of these poems tell stories, or tell you part of

a story and let you choose how to finish it for yourself. A bomb goes off in the London Underground. What was happening five minutes before? A ship is raised from the seabed where it has lain for hundreds of years since it sank on its maiden voyage. Who last touched the wooden dice found in one of the cabins? Poems can be like detective stories, leaving a trail of clues which spark off your imagination. Even the smallest thing has its story.

You'll notice patterns in many of these poems. There are poems which use rhyme, and those which don't, poems which use repeating refrains or forms like the haiku, and poems which are in free form. You might like to look at these different patterns and think about why they've been used for particular poems. Poems need readers who can bring them alive. Each reader who explores a poem will find something different in it, perhaps something that no one else has ever found before. I hope you'll enjoy the exploration, and your own discoveries.

Helen Dunmore

NIGHT CAT

She's there by the fence
but you mustn't call out,
like a scoop of night
or a water shadow
tense for flight
she'll twist and go,
don't open your mouth —
the moon's so close
that the stars blow out —
you turn   she's gone
leaving that patch
where the moon shone
leaving the empty
dress of night
with the stars picked out
and you alone.

COUNTRY DARKNESS

Now is its time.
Quiet as a vixen,
happiest under the trees
in its own rustling,
country darkness is coming.

Country darkness is coming.
Stand on a wall
high above town in the cold
and watch it fall.
Now is its time.

Now is its time.
Ghostly Kingsway where nobody lives
rolls over and sleeps
in a blanket of leaves,
country darkness is coming

Country darkness is coming,
it was waiting all the time,
smelling of frost and leaves
with night up its sleeves,
now is its time.

Watch it wrapping up nightclubs
in velvety sleep,
watch it stopping
the late-night shopping,
watch it pinch out partygoers'
glittering clothes,
watch it stride into town.
Country darkness is coming —
now is its time.

YELLOW

Think of something yellow.

The sun?
A fat ripe pear
or buttercup petals?

Yellow is butter.
Yellow is custard.
Yellow is yolks.

Yellow has all the answers.
Yellow is like
an advert that twists your eyes
till they light on yellow.

What is yellow?

Nobody answered.
Shakeela smiled
and stroked her yellow
shalwar khameez
so butterly
and buttercuply
that all our fingers turned yellow.

HARBOUR SEAL

Come with the slop of tide up the slipway
come when we're not looking, come suddenly
cutting salt water like butter and
making a ballet of catching
the fishermen's litter,

come while we eat our ice-creams and chatter
and make the glow of it happen
from a flash of recognition,
laugh at us as your nostrils close
in your wet black nose,

come for the French student on exchange
flipping the dictionary for your name
saying 'Seal!' to her friend,
and for the child looking at you
wondering what it's like to be you —

come with your fat wet sides shining
cutting salt water like butter and
making a ballet of catching
our hearts' litter,
and then
go freely again.

BREEZE OF GHOSTS

Tall ship hanging out at the horizon
tall ship blistering the horizon
you've been there so long
your sheets and decks white
in the sun

what wind whispers you in?

Tall ship creaking at the horizon
your captain long gone
your crew in the cabin
drinking white rum
their breath spiralling

what wind breathes you in?

Tall ship tilting to the shoreline
past Spanish palms
tall ship coming in like a swan
in the midday sun

what wind blows you in?

*It is the cool
wind of the morning
stirring my masts
before the sun
burns it to nothing,
they call it
breeze of ghosts.*

WOLF IN MY POCKET

The wolf in my pocket is hungry
because he can't watch the moon,
because the winter snow has melted without
   him,
because the stitching of the sun
on pine tree shadow
is far away and unforgotten,

the wolf in my pocket is angry,
beating a path where the zip
rasps but never opens,
he lollops up and down the lining
catching fluffballs in his claws —
his grey fur is too warm,

the wolf in my pocket howls
as he turns by the seam,
once he had cubs and a cave for them,
now he has none,
once he was cold and alive
on dangerous nights
but now he sleeps and his tongue
hangs out for nothing.

SECRET FOREST

Green-scented
sun-barred
silent
then sounding:

boom of wind on the crown of the pines
murmur of bees on blossom of balsam
whine of midges clouding the fern.

    Wild raspberries
                purple as bruises
                    dissolve in
                      sweetness,

dark
dry
still-bodied pines
make the wind sigh

while their arms
scratch the sky.

From airy platforms
they lean out tossing
their waves of green

and the line of hills
gallops on
dwarfing, dwindling
to tundra and lichen.

but here
sun-barred
bark smells of cinnamon,

a water-vole
        head-down
                slips
under the loggers' bridge

busy

and quick.

NIGHT LORRIES

unzipping miles
of white lane-lines
approaching
faster than owls

gap-toothed lorries
spangled like castles
round the black hole
of night cargoes

headlights full on
wheel-towers
drumming the crown
of the fast lane

and they're gone, making
that thin finishing whine

red lights
in your mirror
not even braking

LORRIES BEHIND

The teeth of lorries in the driving mirror
the breath of lorries on the rear window

the hiss of lorries waiting to shoulder by,
the throb of diesel, the air-brake sigh

the hot shimmer in the driving mirror.
Lorries behind. Too close. *Look at that smile*.

SAD LORRIES

Wayside sad lorries
jackknifed, slipshod

one wheel on the road
nobody's rig

halfway to the wrecker's

one wheel on the road
lorries lying low

two days
with small corrugate smiles

they wait for the crusher
to wipe out the miles

THE CUCKOO GAME

It starts with breaking into the wood
through a wave of chestnut leaves.

I am grey as a spring morning
fat and fuzzy as pussy willow,

all around I feel them simmering
those nests I've laid in,

like burst buds, a hurt place
lined for the young who've gone

unfledged to the ground.
There they splay, half-eaten

and their parents see nothing
but the one that stays.

This is the weather that cuckoos love:
the breaking of buds,

I am grey in the woods, burgling
the body-heat of birds,

riding the surf of chestnut flowers
on spread feathers.

I love the kiss of a carefully-built nest
in my second of pausing —

this is the way we grow
we cuckoos,

if you think cuckoos never come back
we do. We do.

WHOOPER SWANS

They fly
      straight-necked and barely white
        above the bruised stitching of clouds
        above wind and the sound of storms
        above the creak of the tundra
         the howl of weather
          the scatter
           and wolfish gloom
             of sleet icing their wings,

they come
    on their strong-sheathed wings
      looking at nothing
        straight down a freezing current of light,
        they might
          astonish a sleepy pilot
            tunnelling his route above the Arctic,

his instruments darken and wink
    circling the swans
      and through his dull high window at sunrise
      he sees them
        ski their freezing current of light
          at twenty-seven thousand feet
            past grey-barrelled engines
              spitting out heat
                across the flight of the swans,

and they're gone

                    the polar current sleeking them down
                        as soon as he sees them.

RUSSIAN DOLL

When I held you up to my cheek you were cold
when I came close to your smile it dissolved,

the paint on your lips was as deep
as the steaming ruby of beetroot soup

but your breath smelled of varnish and pine
and your eyes swivelled away from mine.

When I wanted to open you up
you glowed, dumpy and perfect

smoothing your dozen little selves
like rolls of fat under your apron

and I hadn't the heart to look at them.
I knew I would be spoiling something.

But when I listened to your heart
I heard the worlds inside of you spinning
like the earth on its axis spinning.

SNOW QUEEN

Long long I have looked for you,
snowshoeing across the world
across the wild white world

with my heart in my pocket
and my black greased boots
to keep the cold out,

past cathedrals and pike marshes
I've tracked you,
so long I have looked for you.

In your star-blue palace
I wandered and could not find you
in your winter garden
I picked icicles,

my fingers burned on your gate
of freezing iron
I have the pain
of it yet on my palm,

through clanging branches
and black frost-fall
I dared not call

so I slide above worlds of ice
where the fishes kiss

and the drowned farmer
whips on his cart
through bubbles of glass

and his dogs prance
at the tail-end, frozen
with one leg cocked
and their yellow urine

twined in thickets of ice.
I stamp my boot
and the ice booms.

I have looked so long
I am wild and white
as your creatures, I might
be one of your own.

THE BONES OF THE VASA

(The VASA was a royal Swedish ship of the sixteenth century. She sank on her maiden voyage.)

I saw the bones of the *Vasa* knit in the moonlight
I heard her hull creak as the salt sea slapped it
I smelled her tar and her freshly-planed pine,

there were rye loaves slung up on poles for drying
there were herrings in barrels and brandy-wine
and every plank in her body was singing,

off-duty sailors were throwing the dice
while the royal flag cracked at the mast
and the wind grew strong and the clouds flew past

Oh the *Vasa* never set sail down the salt sea's stream
down the salt stream for a second time
while the midsummer islands waited like secrets,

the King's *Vasa* flew down like a swan
parting the waves and the sea's furrow
parting that long road where the drowned roll
and the tide rules the kingdom of no one.

THE BRAGGART AND THE PUDDING

It came in the night.

                                    Nobody saw it.
                                    Nobody
                                    made it.

By dawn it was steaming
among the horse-mushrooms
astonishing
the fog-damp sheep
and the children,

                    rolling and boiling
                    fruit-studded
                    spice-smoking
                    fuming and gleaming
                    glossily steaming
                    sugar sweet
                    citrus sharp
                    pudding

so big you could not tie your arms around it
so big it would put out the fire in your kitchen
so big there would be enough for everyone.

                          'I'll have it,'
              said the Braggart
              and put his boot on the pudding.

The people drew back
and laid their hands over the mouths of the
  children
and looking at the pudding
one by one
they muttered

      'OK you take it' 'that's fine'
          'think nothing of it' 'you take it' 'forget it'
          'can't eat rich food anyway' 'haven't the
          stomach for it'
          'good on you' 'Braggart you take it'

      So the Braggart took it.
      With his bare hands he took it
      and raced off palming it
      between his hands with the
      steam slapping them

      his red red hands
      long and pointed as flames.

The Braggart took the world of the pudding

              to his secret place

                  to his cave of bones

            where he kept his knife
              and his steel
            and his white spoon
            made from a bull's thigh
              bone.

So.

He rolls up his sleeves
braces his legs like a wrestler
snorting
he rocks forward
and so
he advances upon the
   pudding.

> Oh the Braggart
> the great man
> he went to war
> upon a pudding

It was so delicious he could
   have wept
as his spoon oozed through
   the crust
and out came
a nestful of eggs
warm and brown
flour fine-milled as silk
a thin current of honey
out came blackstrap
   molasses
ginger-stem
and a full bottle
of brandy-wine.

It was so delicious he could
   have laughed
as he dug his way to the
   heart
of that marvellous pudding
through mazes of grapes
through candied groves
of orange and lemon.

Time passed.
The sheep ate their way
 through the fog.
The people thought that one
 morning the pudding
would come again
and the children listened.

Towards night they began to
 hear a sound
neither like weeping nor
 laughing.
Everyone fell silent —
was it the Braggart?

It was the pudding
the marvellous pudding
the pudding speaking

rolling and boiling
fruity and fuming
stuck with cloves
and steaming with spices

it spoke in a voice
as rough as the iron
pot it had boiled in:

'come on! come on!'
the pudding taunted
its bleary punch-drunk
belching opponent
his eyes half-closed
as he staggered reeling
across the ring
squinting at nothing
'come on! come on!'
taunted the pudding.

'There's your man!'
>	The people whisper
>	smelling the wind
>	which is heavy with pudding.

The children hold hands

>	and run on tiptoe

>>	as close as they dare
>>	to the secret place
>>	to the cave of bones

>>	where the pudding swells
>>	where the Braggart slumps

>>	and the children laugh
>>	as loud as they dare

>>	and the children yell
>>	as loud as they can:

YES! THERE'S YOUR MAN!

MARKS

WATERMARK

Hold me up to the light
        and see me
in everything you write.

        FINGERPRINTS

        Fingerprints
            patterning history
                brief and
            unique
                    as
                      whirling
                        snowflakes.

STAIN

Lies.
        A slow stain
        darkening
        friendship.

        SIGNATURE

        Loops and
        downstrokes
                building
        a house for your name.

ROPER

Roper says he's king of this land
he's drunk as a skunk and he speaks as he finds
he'll eat swan for his dinner and steal his own
   crown

*   fly down*

would you take Roper for love or for money
could you sweeten Roper with a hive-full of
   honey
could you make yourself laugh at what Roper
   finds funny?

*   fly down*

Roper has quarrelled the sun from the sky
he eats till he belches and if you ask why
he roars he's been feasting on elephant pie

*   fly down*

Roper is much and Roper is many
Roper is hungry for anything any
old fiver or oner or dollar or penny

*   fly down*

Roper is getting his turn one day soon
Roper is writing the laws and the rules
and Roper-studies for primary schools

*   fly down*

Roper says he'll be king of this land
and Roper will. If you look at his hand
you can read the lines there. They just say AND

fly
down.

JIM BEAN

Jim Bean is our budgerigar.
He loves to look at himself in the mirror

and to fly right to the top of the umbrella
plant in the corner of the room
and make it shiver.

There he waits with his head on one side
for the rest of the forest

which he knows is quivering
behind the door

putting out fresh green leaves like palms
for him to climb on.
Soon it will join him.

Jim Bean, Jim Bean
does not choose even to tongue his own name

but he can whistle and sing
and rock himself on his branch sweetly.

He knows there's a syllable missing
when we only call 'Jim! Jim!'

or when we forget to turn on the tap
at full gush so he can imitate it,

and he can imitate the washing machine
or the wheeze and whirr when the fridge goes
   on.

In the mornings he's full of it —
the rushing kettle, the grill-flame, the scrape
of our chairs. But he prefers water.

He would not lose one syllable of it.
Jim Bean. Jim Bean.

JIM BEAN AND THE SWIFTS

Jim Bean doesn't yet know he is waiting —
he is too young —

but the sky is paling more and more each evening
and by the time he has stripped
three packets of millet
the swifts will come.

Jim Bean from his window will be party
to their wild parties on the wing
and their sudden mating,

he will catch the cut of their flight
their scissor-like flings

and he will sing,
Jim Bean.

JIM BEAN AND THE DARKNESS OF HEAVEN

(for Philip Gross)

The Russian Academic Choir sings
and Jim Bean listens.

Too blissful even to peck at his millet
he fattens his feathers
he fluffs and nestles
under the sheltering wing
of this bird he can scarcely imagine

and the Russian Academic Choir sings
like the darkness of heaven.

CHRISTMAS CAVES

A draught like a bony finger
felt under the door

but my father swung the coal scuttle
till the red cave of the fire roared

and the pine-spiced Christmas tree
shook out plumage of glass and tinsel.

The radio was on but ignored,
greeting 'Children all around the world'

and our Co-op Christmas turkey
had gone astray in the postal system —

the headless, green-gibletted corpse
revolved in the sorting-room

its leftover flesh
never to be eaten.

Tomorrow's potatoes rolled to the boil
and a chorister sang like a star

glowing by the lonely moon —
but he was not so far,

though it sounded like Bethlehem
and I was alone in the room

with the gold-netted sherry bottle
and wet black walnuts in a jar.

FOR FRANCESCA

it's so early in the morning

the cobweb
stretched between the gateposts
is not yet broken

couples
stir in their beds
and sigh and smile
and the hard
words of the day
are not yet spoken

it's so early in the morning

the street lamps go out
one by one
the small stars disappear
and your life
has barely begun

it's so early in the morning

PLAYGROUND HAIKU

Everyone says our
playground is overcrowded
but I feel lonely.

BABY ORANG-UTAN

Bold flare of orange —
a struck match
against his mother's breast

he listens to her heartbeat
going *yes yes yes*

FREE-WHEELING

I race downhill
through hoops of shadow
freewheeling
tyres blazing,

I come down
slow as a yawn
in a mash of blood
on the tarred kerbstone,
my blood all new
on the yellow line.

Heads hide the sun,
say I am bleeding,
I suck my lip
and I can't feel it,
my breath is quick
as feathers flying,
I hear the wheels
tick round and round,
I hear the bike
freewheeling on.

LEMON SOLE

I lay and heard voices
spin through the house
and there were five minutes to run
for the snow-slewed school bus.

My mother said they had caught it
as she wiped stars from the window —
the frost mended its web
and she put her snow-cool hand to my forehead.

The baby peeked round her skirts
trying to make me laugh
but I said my head hurt
and shut my eyes on her and coughed.

My mother kneeled
until her shape hid the whole world.
She buffed up my pillows as she held me.
'Could you eat a lemon sole?' she asked me.

It was her favourite
she would buy it as a treat for us.
I only liked the sound of it
slim, holy and expensive

but I said 'Yes, I will eat it'
and I shut my eyes and sailed out
on the noise of sunlight, white sheets
and lemon sole softly being cut up.

HEDGEHOG HIDING AT HARVEST IN HILLS ABOVE MONMOUTH

Where you hide
    moon-striped grass ripples like tiger skin
where you hide
    the dry ditch rustles with crickets

where you hide
    the electricity pylon saws and sighs
    and the combine harvester's headlight
    pierces the hedges

where you hide
    in your ball of silence
    your snorts muffled
    your squeaks and scuffles
    gone dumb

        a foggy moon sails over your head,
        the stars are nipped in the bud

where you hide
> you hear the white-faced owl hunting
> you count the teeth of the fox.

WATERLILY

Under the surface
          information
          waits

    stored in a flower

    slim
    tight-budded

    it rises

    pearly
    bright-budded
    it flexes

one petal turns over
waking the others

yellow unpleats

      like the iris
      of a tiger

      like the iris of a tiger
      it widens

      and leaps.

MY LIST OF NIGHT

My list of night begins
on a wet black forecourt in the rain.
Wind slices the puddles.
The automatic doors punch shut
just missing my feet.

My list of night goes on
with my jacket not keeping me warm,
while someone picks carnations out of a bucket
because they're hospital visiting.
The wind gets its hands on my kidneys.
I've stood still too long.

My list of night likes hospitals
because there's always something going on,
you can go in and get a coffee
and pretend you're waiting to be seen.
Sometimes I fall asleep, then jerk
as an army marches after me
in the quick black shoes of the nurse.

My list of night knows when to be frightened
and when to run. There are times
when it's better not to ask questions
or look like someone who asks questions,
times you learn to move on.
It is 3 a.m. and here I am
breathing fast in the shadow of a warehouse
hoping they won't come.

My list of night goes on till morning
which is always the coldest time.
By now I'm on my feet dreaming
as the streetlamps flap at shadows
and the foxes go home. I've nearly got
   something
warm and sweet in my hands. Polystyrene
that squeaks on my teeth, tea
and a sandwich, steam on the window writing
my list of night.

HERRING GIRL

*See this 'un here, this little bone needle,
he belonged to the net menders.*

I heard the crackle in your throat
like fishbone caught there, not words.

And this other 'un, he's wood, look,
you said to the radio interviewer

and I couldn't see the fine-fashioned needle
or the seams on your face,

but I heard the enormous hiss of herring
when they let the tailboard down

and the buyers bargaining
as the tide reached their boots,

I heard the heave of the cart, the herring girls'
laugh as they flashed their knives —

*Such lovely voices we all had
you ought t'have heard us
singing like Gracie Fields
or else out of the hymn book.*

Up to your elbows, you gutted
your pile of herring. The sludge

was silver, got everywhere.
Your hands were fiery and blooded.

from the slash and the tweak and the salt
and the heap of innards for the gulls.

*I'd put a little bit o' bandage round these fingers
— you can see where they been nicked,*

*we had to keep going so quick
we could never wear gloves.*

THE BURIED MEDAL

A man in a hole in the road found a coin.
Was it gold, was it a lucky one?
Would he keep it for his grandchildren
or make it the Queen's treasure trove?

It was not money. It was a medal,
cheaply made, not of costly metal,
cleanly made with a clear outline
of the head of an old woman.

Of course, he knew, *it's Victorian*.
He found out the medals were given
to the inmates of the local orphanage —
one for each of the children.

They are still remembered, those children
with shaved heads walking in line,
getting yesterday's bread for breakfast
and glad of it. Never alone

for to be alone was dangerous
in the Eller Road Orphanage
and every child would earn a medal
simply for staying alive

for staying in line and breathing
that year the old Queen stuck to her throne
and wrote letters to her daughter in Russia
about keeping on top of things for ever.

THE BUTCHER'S DAUGHTER

Where have you been, my little daughter
out in the wild weather?

*I have met with a sailor, mother,
he has given me five clubs for juggling
and says I must go with him for ever.*

Oh no, my treasure
you must come in and stay for ever
for you are the butcher's daughter.

Where have you been, my little daughter
in the winter weather?

*I have met a man of war, mother,
he has given me four hoops to dance through
and he says I must love him for ever.*

Oh no, my treasure
you must come in and shut the door
for you are the butcher's daughter.

Where have you been, my little daughter,
out in stormy weather?

*I have met with a prince, mother,
he has given me three promises
and I must rule his heart for ever.*

Oh no, my treasure
you must give back his promises
for you are the butcher's daughter.

Where have you been, my little daughter
in the wild of the weather?

*I have spoken to a wise man, mother,
who gave me knowledge of good and evil
and said I must learn from him for ever.*

Oh no, my treasure
you have no need of his knowledge
for you are the butcher's daughter.

Where have you been, my little daughter
out in the summer weather?

*I have met with a butcher, mother,
and he is sharpening a knife for me
for I am the butcher's daughter.*

SMALL DIP IN THE STONE

Small dip in the stone
where we put our fingers in passing
and stand, steadying
the day that's gone
now that we're home.

and just before we call out
or kick off our boots
or look up at starlings in thousands
dancing before they roost
and the evening sky white
as an apple's inside,

just before the door opens
or the day outside closes
before we are out of the wind
eating and drinking
we touch the stone.

It was here before we came,
small dip in the stone,
so we put our fingers in it
where the day's rain has run out of it,
it is our own
small dip in the stone.

ME MISSING A PARTY

I was on my way to a party.

It was just the usual crowded tube platform —
wind like a hairdryer full on
and a train coming,

the girl beside me twisted in slow motion
from the keyboard of the chocolate machine
her skirt blew out and blew in —

they said she was catching the tube home
after two hours' overtime,

she wasn't going to the party
but she got written into the story.

I wasn't really watching her.
I was playing with the thought of a Wispa
but my mind was elsewhere.

*And when you heard the explosion
what did you feel? Did you run?*

I never heard the explosion.
I was thinking of the party
when someone picked me up and threw me.

The thing was, I couldn't get my breath.
My face was in something red.

*But when you knew it was a bomb
was there much panic? Did you hear screaming
or did people stay calm?*

The train must've come in
but the doors didn't open.

They must've missed it by a minute
because it only took a minute

I had my face in something red
but it was the girl's leg.

The doors stayed shut, that was the strangest
thing —
all those faces staring.

*First reports suggest a small bomb
hidden behind the chocolate machine.*

The rest is history
or me missing a party.

THE PELTING RAIN

Poor Johnny
he's lost it again
he's out trying to find it
in the pelting rain

the wild woods are thrashing
the weather's insane
trees double over

jays scream for shelter
the lamppost flashes
signals for rescue

and Johnny'd better
skid helter-skelter
for safe haven —

but he's gone again
poor Johnny
looking for sunshine
in the pelting rain.

THE CATHERINE WHEEL WHINGE

It's time to hammer in the nail
light the blue paper and retire,
wait for the catherine wheel to fail.

You hit the fence to make her go,
see how she hisses on her nail
she only comes to spoil your show.

You're sick of fireworks that don't fire
and if the catherine wheel won't go
you'll soon fire her. Let her retire.

WHITE MOON

White moon

        sheeted by cloud
        slurring the little fields,
        when will you press them
        with owl-soft heaviness
        so that they yield
        harvests of oak shadow,

white moon

        the cloud-turreted sky
        hurries towards midnight,
        your flakes thicken and fall
        as we wait in the lane
        looking up and guessing
        where you will come.

THE GREENFIELD GHOST

The greenfield ghost is not much of a ghost,
it is a ghost of dammed-up streams,
it is a ghost of slow walks home
and sunburn and blackberry stains.

The greenfield ghost is not much of a ghost.
It is the ghost of low-grade land,
it is the ghost of lovers holding hands
on evening strolls out of town.

The greenfield ghost is not much of a ghost.
It is the ghost of mothers at dusk calling,
it is the ghost of children leaving their dens
for safe houses which will cover them.

THAT VIOLET-
HAIRED LADY

That violet-haired lady, dowager-
humped, giving herself so many
smiles, taut glittering smiles,
smiles that swallow the air in front of her,
smiles that cling to shop-mirrors
and mar their silvering, smiles
like a spider's wrinklework
flagged over wasteland bushes —

she's had so many nips and tucks,
so much mouse-delicate
invisible mending. Her youth
squeaks out of its prison —
the dark red bar of her mouth
opening and closing.
She wants her hair to look black,
pure black, so she strands it with violet,
copperleaf, burgundy, rust —
that violet-haired lady, dowager-
humped, giving herself
so many smiles, keeping the light on.

WINTER HAIKU

Christmas in prison,
barbed wire glitters in searchlights —
a fence made of stars.

Ice on the windows,
tangerines peeled in one curl
under the bedclothes.

Policemen pour out
of a riot van's siren
chasing the silence.

Two plastic reindeer
a shopping-bag of holly
a mouthful of frost.

The houses are shut,
no one walks the empty streets —
has there been a death?

Left out milk bottles
suddenly find company
— holey silver top.

RICHARD THE BAD, RICHARD THE GOOD

Richard the Bad was a Staffordshire bull terrier
with eyes like wildfire. Richard was a warrior,

if he spotted a poodle or dachshund or tyke
he was after it before you could say knife.

He ought to be kept locked up, muzzled and
 chained,
if you let him free he'd only do it again.

Richard the Good was a Staffordshire bull
 terrier:
my mother's dog, a bit of a worrier

after dark if she was late home.
He never liked her going out alone

but with him at her side my mother had the
 freedom of Manchester,
no park was too dark for her and her
 Staffordshire bull terrier.

POMEGRANATES DO NOT FEEL PAIN

Fasten your face onto its flesh
and suck each bead through your teeth,

dig out the pips with a tarnished teaspoon
while you sit on top of the washing machine,

squeeze half-moons on a lemon-squeezer
(make sure you're wearing a white T-shirt)

or stab your pomegranate with a whelk pin —
pomegranates do not feel pain.